Philosophical questions for kids?
...

What is love?

Love is one of the most loved concepts by philosophers, and it can be defined as an expansion of the heart toward another human being (our family, friends ...) , and that's how some philosophers explain it :

For PLATO 'Greek philosopher' : *"**love is any general desire towards the good things and to happiness**"* which mean when you decide to eat an apple instead of an orange, it's because you love apples more than oranges but, that love is very different from your love to your parents or your friends, but three of this sensation are love because you have a **desire towards them**, that's what PLATO said not me . 😊

But there is an other friend who has an other opinion :
   our friend **SPINOZA** ' a Dutch philosopher' ፥ who thinks that love is :
' nothing but a joy accompanied by an external cause '
   in other words for SPINOZA whenever you feel happy , (and we will comeback to happiness) about something , that means , you love that thing ,whatever it is a person , an animal , a toy , a place ….

and we have an other opinion here from **Aristotle ,** who is also a greek philosopher who explain that *"self-love is a prerequisite to loving others"* which mean in order to love others you should before that love yourself , because for him if you don't love yourself you can't love others .

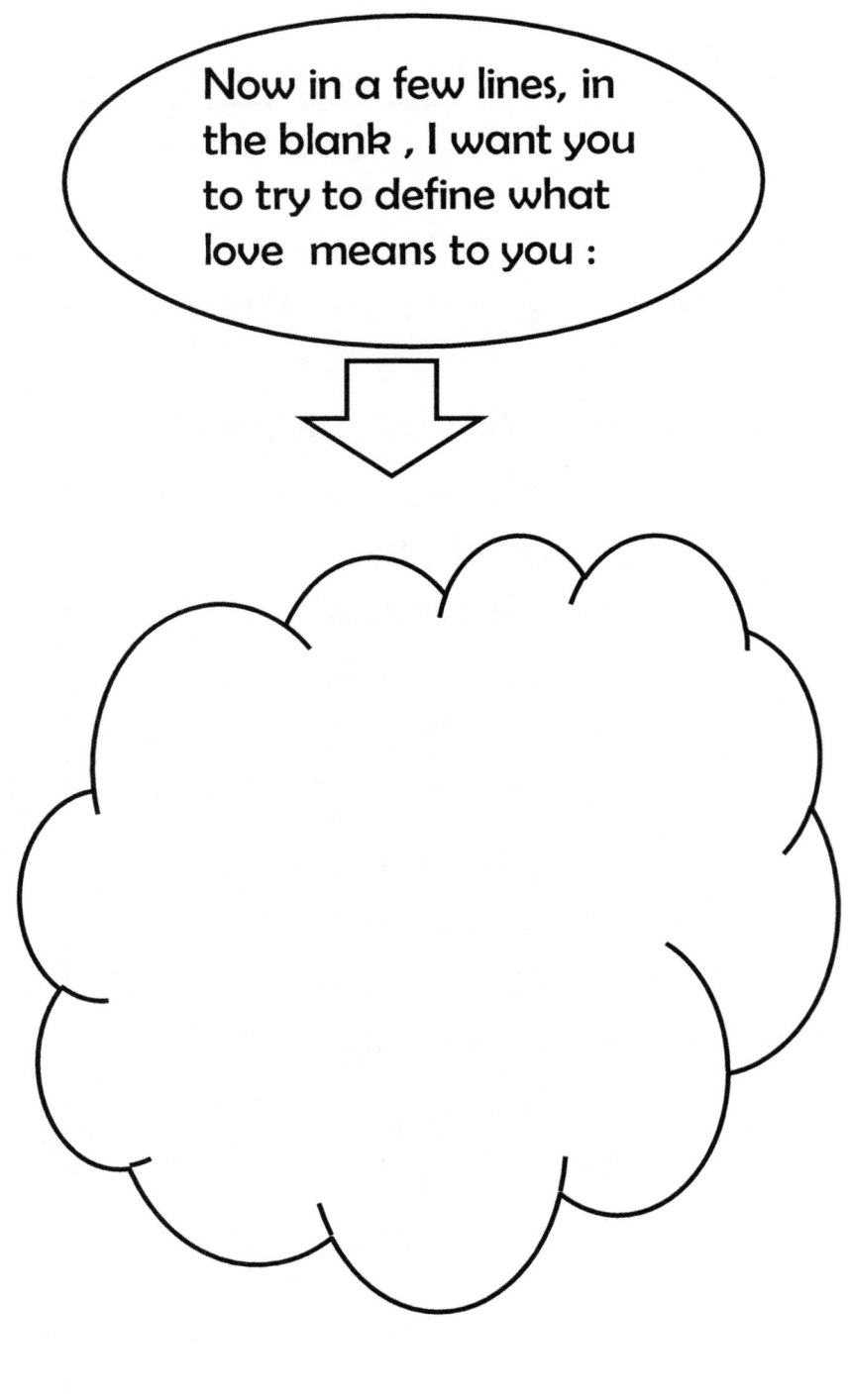

When we become adult?

Becoming an adult happens step by step in life , and it's not necessarily about age , it's more about experience, so if someone is more 'adult' than you, it's because he had more experience than you in life.

a person becomes an adult when they can make decisions for themselves they way a loving parent would make decisions for them.

For example, a loving parent would be happy to give a healthy child a bowl ice cream after dinner, but would not let the child eat a half gallon of it for dinner. If a person is suffering from disease , a loving parent would seek help for them instead of thinking they can handle it on their own. If someone wants something they can't afford, a loving parent says no, save up for it, then buy it. If someone makes a mistake, a loving parent would insist the person apologize, or do what is possible to fix it, but they would also forgive their child, and not continue to punish him. So you become an adult when you decide to treat yourself and love yourself as your loving parent would.

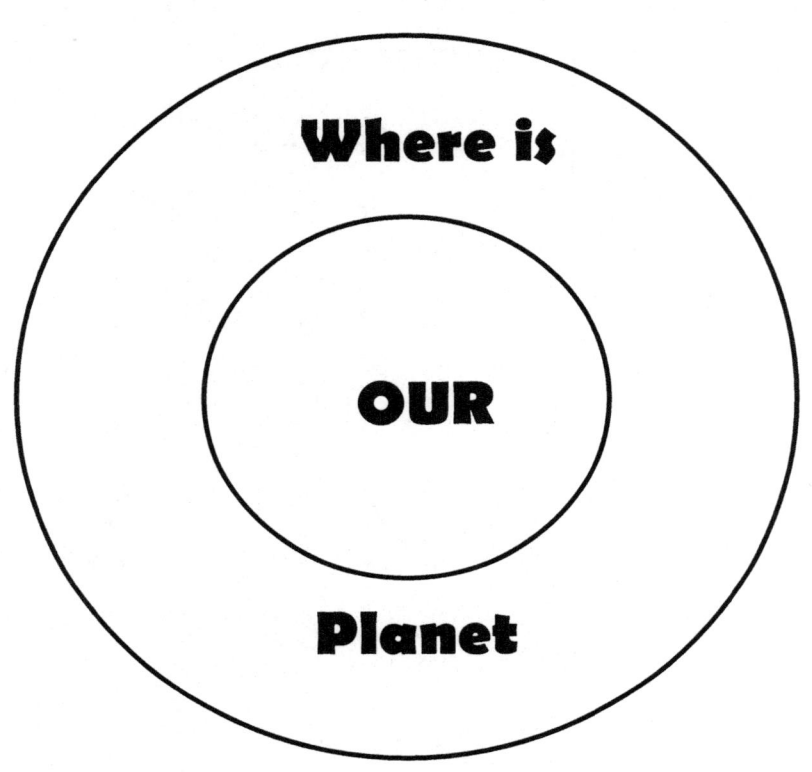

Before you know where is our planet, you should know how the universe is built :
Well, the univers is the collection of all the things that exist in space. In the universe, there are a lot of Galaxies each of them has a lot of stars like the Sun , and with every star there are planets like our planet the earth .

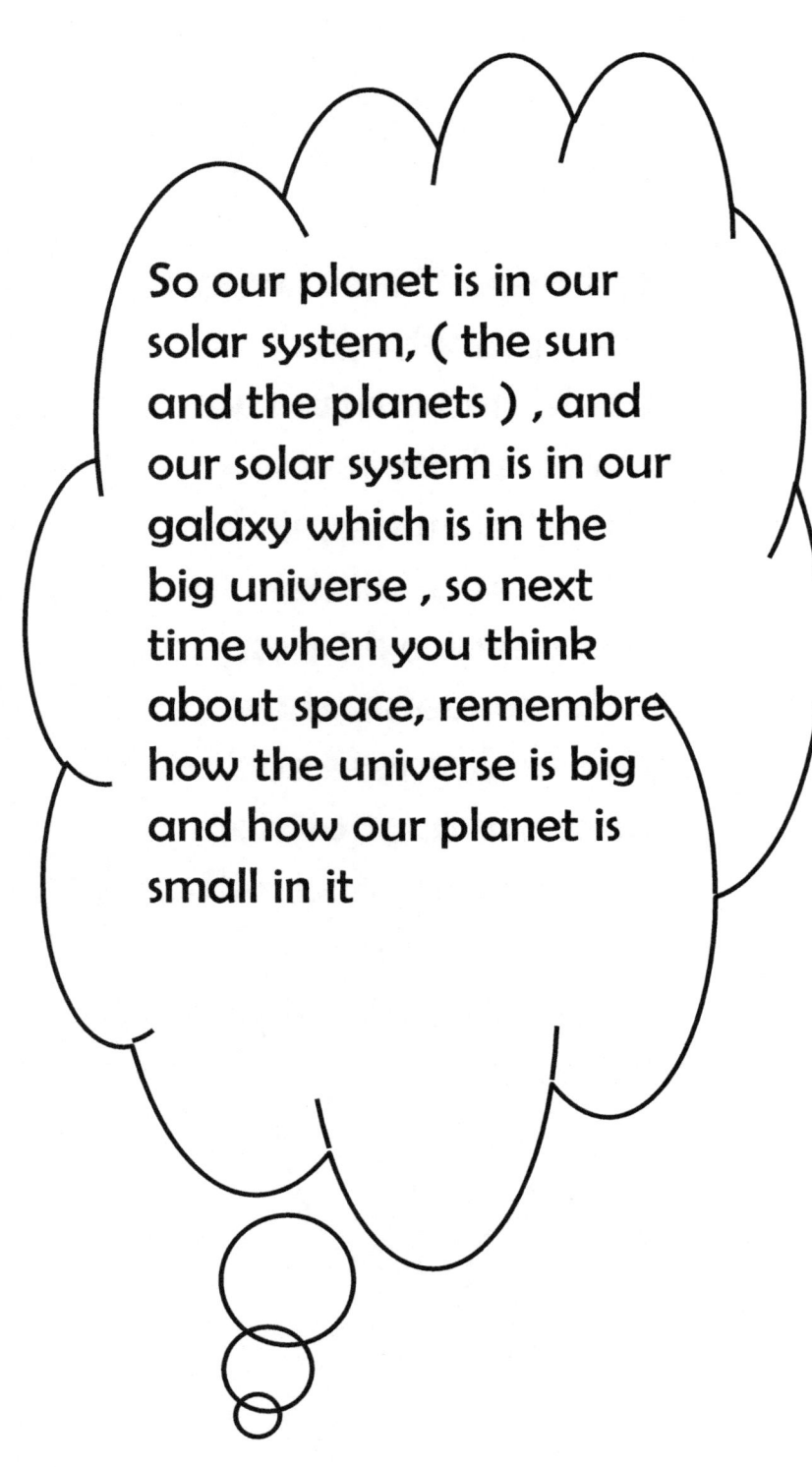

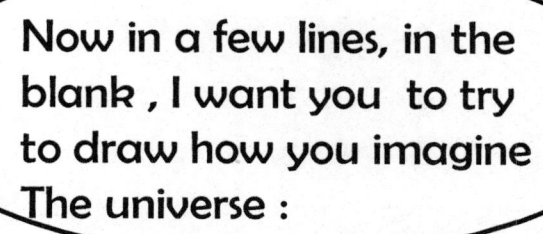

Now in a few lines, in the blank, I want you to try to draw how you imagine The universe :

What is friendship?

Once a man said **"Friendship is born at that moment when one person says to another: "What! You too? I thought I was the only one"** From that example, you can see that friendship is something we share with people that are like us and Friendship is a beautiful relationship between two or more people, a relation of give and take, in friendship we should find love, honesty, loyalty...

Aristotle finds that the perfect friendship is the one in which friends love each other, and they wish good things for each other. ..., but the perfect friendship is where people are friends because they love each other for themselves, not for sake,(These are imperfect friendships, where two friends like each other because they find each other pleasant or useful...) , for Aristotle we should love people for themselves

Happiness is one of the most thought we face in our lives and it's very simple yet it's very difficult to answer it, not because there is no answers but because there is a lot of them.
Everyone has his own answers, his own view, and his own feeling, yes the feelings are very important in happiness, a lot of philosophizes think that to be happy you should feel happy.

Which lead as to another pretty question
What are the feelings? Are emotions controlled by an external effect (for example: we feel happy when we get a surprise from someone), Or it's internal we feel happy when we are happy inside in our souls and minds, are we who makes our lives happy or it's our society, our family, friends .. Or it is our goals, and our Achievements, for example: when you get a good grade you feel happy, but why you can't just be happy , even if you succeed or fail?
Ask yourself this question.

The most important role of 'philosophy' is to ask questions and think about the nature of human thoughts and the universe.
So as Albert Einstein said "never stop asking questions "

A dream is the images, thoughts, and emotions that you experience during sleep, dreams are sometimes very clear, sometimes not, and they can be with good emotions or frightening emotions
But why we dream?
As we said before in this book, there are always multiple answers.

Some scientist think that dreams have no purpose, we dream for just dreaming , others think that our dreams have a purpose, that's mean our dreams helps us to more express our emotions and thoughts that we can't express when we are awake, for example: when you are happy because you get a gift, you start dreaming about that gift , or when you miss someone you start to dream about him, or when you wish something, you start to dream about it, it's your brain express himself in your dreams.

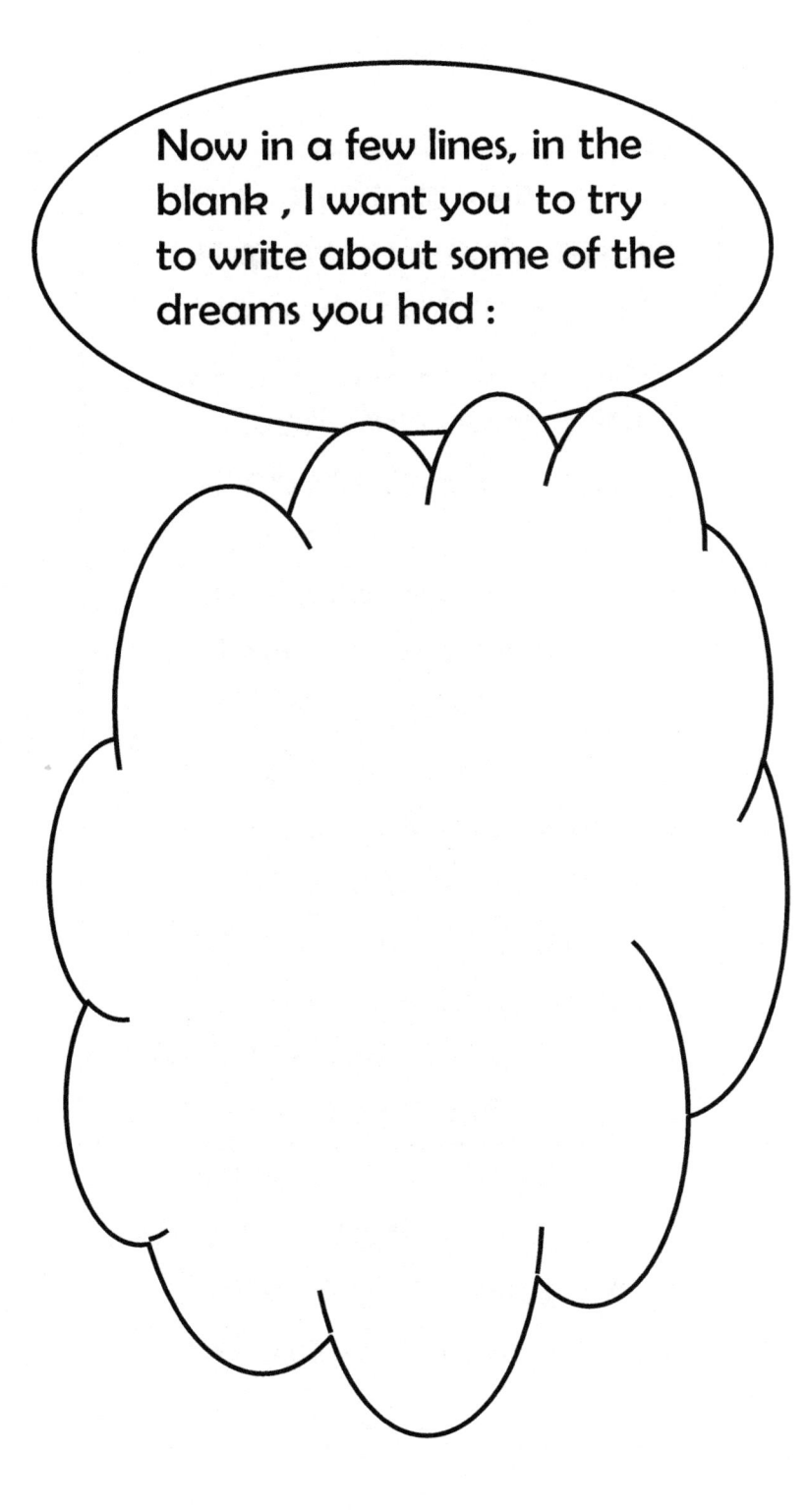

What if everyone looked the same?

Imagine if everyone looked the same, same faces, same eyes, same hairs... Your friends looked the same, your family ...
No difference between people from all the world, same color, same shapes... It may looks good it would be no disputes no wars...

But wouldn't it be boring? Imagine you are about to meet a new person that you haven't seen before, but, you already know how he looks, because everyone looked the same. Have you ever meet a twin? They really look like each other , Imagine if the whole world was like that .

Now in the blank, I want you to try to use all that you have learned in this book, to imagine how the world will be if everybody looks the same, feel free and just imagine and try to think philosophically :

Printed in Great Britain
by Amazon